Leftovers and
Gravy

Ken Waldman

Cyberwit.net
HIG 45 Kaushambi Kunj, Kalindipuram
Allahabad - 211011 (U.P.) India
http://www.cyberwit.net
Tel: +(91) 9415091004
E-mail: info@cyberwit.net

Printed at Thomson Press India Limited

For Lizzie

Grateful acknowledgment is made to the editors of the following journals in which some of these poems, or versions of these poems, first appeared:

Bear Deluxe: "Vitamin X"

Black Buzzard Review: "Cold Pop"

California Poetry Society Quarterly: "Equilibrium"

Chiron Review: "Dear Mother"

Connecticut River Review: "Trailer Park, Yuma"

Convolvulus: "The Past"

CQ: "My Philadelphia"

Eratica: "The Back Surgeon"

eyerhyme: "Orange" "Day-Old Muffin"

Green Hills Literary Lantern: "Brooklyn Weekends" "Her Depression"

Indicting God: "The Elephant Wars"

Lucid Stone: "On Our Way to Wales"

Massachusetts Review: "Bassoon"

Midwest Quarterly: "Beneath Midwest Skies"

New York Quarterly: "In Knowledge"

Pearl: "Frigidity"

Permafrost: "The Fatality of Light"

Poetry Hotel: "Angry Man"

Potato Eyes: "Advice for a Single Mom"

Quarterly West: "Frank Leopold, Jr."

Rag Mag: "Father and Son" "On Depression"

Redneck Review: "Anchorage Classifieds: Jewelry"

Sulphur River Review: "The Vawter Boys" "Family Trees"

Toad Suck Review: "Dolly Jo" "Einsteinian" "Recipe for Foreboding" "Redneck District" "Uncle Floyd's Tongue Recipe"

Wolf Head Quarterly: "The Blue Moon Month"

Wordwrights!: "A Woman Outside Phoenix"

Writers' Forum: "Dear Dad"

Zuzu's Petals Annual: "On 34th Street"

Contents

III

IV

V

I

4024 Woodruff Road

To return, I don't need
to fly to Philadelphia,
take one train downtown,
another to Chestnut Hill,
a bus down Germantown Avenue
to Lafayette Hill,
walk the last three blocks
to the almost half-acre
separated from the neighbors
by small shrubs. Just recall
the family with son
and daughter that lived there once,
the original owners, planters
of azaleas, tenders
of the large sadness
that entered the walls,
lingered, and seeped.
The lawn caught it,
as did the generations
of ants and grasshoppers
that worked the land.
A continent away now,
I picture the plum
and peach that never bore,
fruitless yard without garden
beneath a shabby cloud.
Then I snap fingers
to banish the past.
No chance, so I gaze

beyond the ice, find
that old house anchored
in vast air, the history
I'm asked to write.

Day-Old Muffin

Each bite
of walnut,

bran, date,
carrot shaved

into confetti,
a memory

of earliest
time: sweet

newborn boy
desiring only

milk, love,
a breast.

Brooklyn Weekends

Friday night, mom and dad fought
as we drove the ninety miles to Brooklyn,
where grandmom hugged us and fed us
cookies. When she bent to kiss
my sister and me, her pearl necklace
clinked like an abacus.

Saturday afternoon, mom and grandmom
cooked a roast. Dad slept.
Grandpop took my sister and me
to Coney Island
where we ate hot dogs and roller-coastered.
Grandpop got sick if he rode.

After dinner, the adults played bridge
while my sister and I watched TV
in the bedroom. During commercials,
my sister pranced to the kitchen
modeling grandmom's jewels.
Grandmom always chuckled. Mom, never.

Midday Sunday, pipe in mouth,
grandpop walked us to the car.
Leaving Brooklyn, windows rolled
to keep out the wind, mom and dad bickered
and smoked. In the back, my sister and I
silently counted the miles home.

The Vawter Boys

One afternoon the three
from down the block
ganged up to extort a few quarters
then threatened a real beating
if I told. For two weeks
I submitted until the evening
I broke crying when my father
asked what I did after school.

Following him down the street
to the Vawter yard, where the boys
were playing touch football,
I watched my father tackle Nick,
the youngest, from behind,
slam his body to the grass,
then heard my old man announce
they'd leave his kid alone.

Walking away, straining to match
his big stride, I mimicked
my father's menacing quiet.
He'd taken care of Nick Vawter.
Back home he'd take care of me—
and just that quick I felt
a scary splash, the shark,
and I shoved the swimmer down

like trash into the depths.

Breadwinner

The years the father favored
green cigars thick as thumbs,
he'd light one after dinner,
say *ahhhhh*—not the *ahhhhh*
a doctor or dentist demands
when examining a throat
or mouth, but *ahhhhh*
like a man entering a sauna.
Sipping a second big mug
of instant coffee, he'd commence
to read the sports, the financials,
the front page, and occasionally
puff. Delivering wife and kids
to the happily-ever-after,
the father virtually disappeared,
old man phantom of money and smoke.

Frigidity

The mother had a body
she hated: big breasts,
long legs, hormones
she wanted to smother.
No sex, she muttered,
fists clenching
as she approached
her daughter at play
at the sandbox.
No sex, she hissed,
imagining snapping
the jab to send
her girl flying.

Suburban Chinese Food

Endless tea and crunchy noodles, won ton soup,
egg rolls, spare ribs, two from Column A
and two from Column B—father insistent
on sweet and sour pork, butterfly shrimp;
mother always undecided before settling
on moo goo gai pan, crab egg foo yong—
my sister and I ordered fizzy, pink
Shirley Temples that came with plastic
straws and those miniature umbrellas
which we unraveled at the hinge
for the thin roll of Chinese newspring
obscure as all history.

China Garden, Ocean Kai, Twin Dragon,
Golden Wok: Do the names matter?
Oblivious to MSG and saccharin, to globs
of white rice, to the bad taste
of canned peas, to our hosts' past,
we returned. The fortune cookies
never revealed the truth:
Two messy adolescences—
an even messier divorce.
After father paid, we rode
the expressways home.

Teenage Snacker

Going to bed full,
waking 3 A.M., belly
emptied by the vacuum
that sucked the life
from that house, he couldn't
shake a strange dark hunger

for stealth, so tiptoed
downstairs, crept
to the kitchen, found
sweet relief by grabbing
dad's last doughnut,
mother's box of holes.

Family Trees

My mother's junipers—
how she'd gab on,
bored suburban matron,
too many failures.

My father's peach—
lone back yard
fruit tree, a hard
par five never reached.

My sister's dogwood—
she watered, pruned, fed
that plant to death.
Her love did no good.

My grandfather's chestnuts—
to keep the family
in money
we sawed the trunks.

My oak—
up high I built a house,
struck a pose,
kept the books.

My Philadelphia

Off the turnpike's cloverleaf,
Plymouth Meeting's busy spillage
of concrete ribbons tied Conshohocken
to Blue Bell, Germantown, Ambler,
Skippack, Lafayette Hill, a Wissahickon
of tributaries, bridges, drives,
expressways with names like 202
and 309. Home was somewhere near
the jackhammer of construction
off our Chemical Road shortcut,
near the Jewish country club's
golf course we carpooled by, near
the smoke of an industrial park
beside the abandoned limestone quarry
that told and retold our story.

II

Dream Week

Monday: My mother's in
a box that's flying,
wood wings flapping. Noise
like a wind machine.
A cold voice:
You must go home.

Tuesday: Nobody home.
A long knife's in
my hand. A voice:
Chop chop—butcher flying—
chop chop—butcher machine.
Suddenly, lots of noise.

Wednesday: A humming noise.
My father's bringing home
a large, shiny machine
half-hidden in
a box. *We're flying*
now, he says, low voice.

Thursday: A voice
making hooting noises
like an owl. A bird's flying
into the moon. Home—
the letters appear in
code on a machine.

Friday: A machine
with blades. A voice
says somebody's in
trouble. I hear noises.
A woman gasps: *To go home*
one must go flying.

Saturday: A table flying
in the wind. A sewing machine
soaring past. A home
being ripped by storm. Voices
I almost catch in the noise.
Glass broken, I look in.

Sunday: *I'm flying*, I say, voice
high over machine noises.
Heading home, they say, cutting in.

Fairbanks Moon

Lopsided moon, watch where you're going—
    wobble through space.

Foolish moon, unicycle in wind—
    caught by a cloud.

Insane moon, howl at the cats—
    play tricks on warts.

Moody moon, work the shadows—
    fancy the sun.

Mean moon, loaded on darkness—
    don't hit me.

Tipsy moon, out past dawn—
    come home quietly.

Noon moon, I can tell—
    you're changing.

Dredge Song

Past seventy, I've been manufactured,
transported, assembled, disassembled, barged,
railed, shipped, hauled, reassembled. I've been
nailed, hammered, stomped on, strolled through.
I've seen drunks and thieves, thugs and saints.
I've seen the best and worst mechanics
on earth. But mostly I've seen ordinary men
doing extraordinary work
on even more extraordinary land. I've seen
men go deaf as they pile on the hours
shift after shift. I've seen men go crazy
from the noise, the mosquitoes, the schemes.
I've seen the most gorgeous long mornings,
the most improbable dusks, summer light
anyone would envy. I've seen a stack
of dark frozen Decembers, their spectacular auroras.
And I've seen big gold nuggets, small gold rocks,
what must have been a ton of glittery flakes
and sparkly dust, shinier than the most beautiful
eyes. All that—and more—has passed through me.
I've been disassembled, trucked, reassembled
back to where I'd once been, here
by the river. Watch close. Listen well.
There's true dirt to be shaken in pans.
Make the gravel rattle. Let the light stuff go.
Dip once more. Gently swirl. See what's beneath.

Boxes

for Gene

Say your life's the story
of 57 small hardwood boxes.

So you add a 58th,
calling it your apartment.

So you add a 59th,
calling it your day job.

So you add a 60th,
calling it the endless

ticking, ticking
of dissatisfaction.

So you juggle those boxes,
adding a 61st,

the future, which makes
you fumble them all.

In the brokenness
of those dropped boxes,

you set up an easel
to paint every sorry sliver

and shape on canvas
after canvas after canvas.

In Memory of Ian Pounds

1

He abhorred the easy shortcut, the quick
fix. How apt he took to building, writing,
making his life in one inhospitable
climate after another. Incorrigible
Yankee, muscular Alaskan, such biting
wit, how he'd skip sleep to tend to a sick
boy, or friend, or student, or to trick
his mind into another self. Fighting
man, gentleman, madman, a horrible
husband one moment, a most beautiful
human the next. And always the writing
which delighted, frustrated. Harshest critic
of his own work, he sought tough perfection.
What he left: sad, unfinished collections.

2

I'd never once seen
a more quiet stubbornness.
No fools suffered, he

preferred the hard way,
or, better, the impossible way.
Useless to argue with him.
No fools suffered, he'd rather
die than take it easy. So headstrong,
smart, passionate. So ornery.

Frank Leopold, Jr.

Mostly he wishes his dad wasn't
redneck bastard, his mom wasn't useless,
his stupid life wasn't criss-crossed
with grief for losses he couldn't name,
wishes he could accept the long fingers
that ought to be stubs, the big red curls
that ought to be shorn, days and nights
that cry dry storms. Recently busted
at work for downloading porn,
he wishes and nothing and everything could
change, this dusty spring could be
the same as his recurring dream:
riding his bike in front of a speedy truck,
somehow flying over traffic unharmed.
Frank Leopold Jr., age twenty-three,
decides to reopen the book
he's just set down. And so begins
Crime and Punishment for the fourth time.

A Woman Outside Phoenix

Ten years after the divorce
from a man you'd still like
to knife, you've kept his name.
Why? For extra protection
from the slick Hispanic men
who maintain the condominium grounds?
For proof your twenty-year marriage
worked, the split never happened?
Listen. Why aren't you tired of it?
Your children are grown and gone.
You're alone. You keep his name
as a testament of your ruined life:
you're scared of dying with nothing.

Anchorage Classifieds: Jewelry

Perhaps you'll soon realize the poetry
in exchanging your massive 14k bracelet—
the shiny huge love hoop that jangled
gold against your bony right wrist—
for firearms. Once you acquire the guns,
perhaps you'll stroke the mouth of one
furtively in your purse, the hate
rising like his dick used to, and imagine
how perhaps you'll spot him one day crossing
Denali at Fourth, so you shoot.
And the shock of the recoil
will burn from fingertip to cunt:
your last stupid bang.

Dolly Jo

Dark ace of the prison poets, Dolly Jo
penned verse that moved. Fists balled tight
as she read, her village English croak
revealed woman's grim revenge—
like Ida, the skinny Yup'ik mouse
married to the failed gold miner, Hans,
a brute who fucked cold and mean
so that Ida's insides sickened
then split from that nightly chore.
One March daybreak she lifted the sharp
butcher knife from a kitchen drawer,
tiptoed to the master bed,
and cut her snoring husband's
genitals, potbelly, throat.
Then she entered his heart.

Redneck District

Plenty of barbwire, prickly weathers.
Summers and winters that last. Springs
and falls that don't. A sun wicked
and sharp as shears. A moon that won't
stay put. Strong backs. Next town down,
monthly dances at the grange hall. Fiddle
and banjo. Kids drinking and smoking
in the parking lot. Cats named Butch.
Dogs named Spike. Pregnant girls.
Gun racks. Frowns. Snarls. Growls.
Far from colleges, theaters, galleries, lawns.
Spits out gristle, mud. Gnaws their own.

Trailer Park, Yuma

When my man kicked me
out, I landed
hard on top of you,
one black cactus
and two orange hearts

tattooed to your belly.
In gritty sheets
we creep like a crab
and a scorpion,
each touch a scrape,

each kiss a claw.
It continues. I love you
like the moonless desert,
like a coyote's bite.
Your tongue stings.

Cold Pop

Ten thousand feet up, the stewardess
asked the child in 12C if she wanted
cold pop. One row back, aisle seat,
the claims adjuster coughed, felt
his chest crack then squeeze, saw
a clouded sun blink bright red, black,
gold. A big click: he lost heart
as a young man when he let Sandy go
and married Ruth, the pretty redheaded
nurse who loved him so much he froze.
Love. How strange to have forgotten
Sandy, the blonde banker's daughter—
his final thought as he fell
out of his seat, groaned, knocked
over the beverage cart. Ice,
liquor bottles, cans of beers, juice,
soda pop flew. The little girl
screamed. The stewardess couldn't
revive the middle-aged man lying
crumpled in the aisle, his face
the blue of weatherbeaten aluminum.

Beneath Midwest Sky

1

Who sees through Dakota fog?
A trucker hauling chickens?
An old man planting wheat?
A farm wife baking cookies?
A piano tuner? A smith?
A child skipping to school?

2

How to endure winter?
Lie inside big river current.
Honor lake squeak and silence.
Forge across prairie at dusk.
Forgive subzero darkness.
Embody ice, snow, stars, light.
Outlast Minnesota stillness.

3

A grandmother sits looking
out an upstairs window.
The land is still the land.
People are still people.
Iowa City. Indeed.
This is no Minneapolis.
Not even Des Moines.

4

Downtown Grand Island,
good god-fearing Nebraskans—
taciturn daddies in suits
and ties—transact bits
of business under wide
honest sun that doesn't
talk back. Or can't.

5

Take a flat, barren
square mile of dust.
Call that place home
from one autumn to the next.
Make bug, dirt, grass,
flowers your family.
Then put down Kansas.

6

Through endless runty hills
the straight rural routes
of southeast Missouri
go up and down steady
and uneven as church
and tavern, crop and work,
plain talk and luck.

Like a Trained Flea

Wearing only a towel, you spend Tuesday
in the studio sipping piña coladas,
outlining a six foot by four foot painting:
pointing at you—the mouth of a gun;
coiling the trigger—a tongue shooting
from the snake
that loops the canvas like a lasso;
in the foreground—a coyote
balanced on a tightrope;
in the background—a clown,
hands nailed to a book.

At 5 A.M., naked, you wake,
bolt to your studio,
pick up a knife,
and slash the painting twenty-six times.

Back in bed, falling
asleep, you hear the ringmaster
announce the next act:
Stupendo the Scribe.

Einsteinian

for Mark Neely

A basic
compendium:
dukes, earls,
forgotten gods,
hard illnesses,
Jack Kerouac,
lost mammals,
noisy owls, pleasure,
quicksand, random
sophisticates, turquoise
underwear, vestigial
wilderness, x-rated
yammering, zippers.

Love Letter to Xavier

Again, be careful. Don't
exit frantically. Go home.
I'll just keep loose, my
never ordinary partner.
Quietly relax: seek
the usual vantage. Wait,
Xavier. You're zen.

Zen: yes, Xavier, wait.
Very ugly times so relax
quietly—perhaps origami.
Now make level keel.
Just inhale here gratefully.
Finally exhale. Divine
contemplative breath? Again.

Orange

Clockwork: the sun
no longer yellow,
not quite red.

A green ball
on a tree
ripens.

Inside
the painted
refrigerator

fruit
for tomorrow's
peeling.

Rinds bit stick
under fingernails.
Juice squirts.

Marmalade on toast
spread thick
with a knife.

Sherbet,
a round scoop, jellybeans
embedded. For dessert

a registered nurse
adds a *J* sound
to her title.

Door hinge.
Dark tinge.
Syringe.

Equilibrium

The instant our eyes
caught, we were held like deer
about to be shot.
And so we froze,
and remain frozen.
It's been one year.

Next month we'll be rising,
rising light
as ghosts—but for our teeth
in each other like ticks.
Dearest beloved, our thirst
for blood pulls.

III

The Back Surgeon

He stepped on a sidewalk crack, which opened. And found himself, knife in hand, sawing through gristle. The words *vertebrae* and *hunger* came. He dropped the blade, picked up one of the small chunks, put it in his mouth, and chewed. Some soft bone, he thought, sucking the hardness. Like an end of an end. And so he worked his way through his mother's remains.

Her Depression

She can't forget
the wounding, the scars.
She hates

her ex. She can't let
him go. Intimate wars
she can't forget—

the slights and debts,
memories like tar.
She hates

him, the divorce a net
she can't escape. His cigars—
she can't forget

the smell. Her pet
peeve these past twenty years.
She hates

the July night they met
forty years back. Shooting stars.
She can't forget.
She hates.

On 34th Street

Late, hurrying toward
the bus stop on Union,
you stepped on a crack,
and were swallowed.
Drills and pumps. Motors.
Grimy mechanics pointed
hoses that gushed acid.
Such acid—you bent, dabbed,
and your top layer of skin
got eaten. Welders aimed
torches. Silvery flames
lit the dirty wall of rock.
Tunnel or hole? Clatter.
You've been here before,
kindergarten, the October
your mother died, lost
to her pills. Mother.
The smell, like a corpse
in a garage. Mother.
You vomited and turned
the corner, now stepping
on crack after crack,
the big city street
open like a mine.

Dear Mother

Did I say our rare long-distance conversations
immediately dry after our hellos and the snap
rundown of weather. I meant die, mother,
die—our conversations die. We have nothing
to share but truths we'd rather not hear.
I live in a perfectly strange trashed cold
little Alaska town somewhere, it seems, between
Jupiter and Mars. You can as little fathom this
and my magnificently absurd work teaching writing
over telephone to village-bound Eskimo collegians
as I can your run-down air-conditioned
South Florida senior's condo, your refusal to see
you have choices. By god, it's pitiful
your 86-year-old mother has twice your energy.
What you do best is shut yourself in and complain.

Last September, searching, I called to ask
about you and dad. In frozen monotone you replied:
I'm no psychiatrist, shrink, whatever you call it—
if you want answers, go talk to your father.
The next month, as usual, you remembered
my birthday with card, check, no news
save you "miss me, think of me, love me." Mother,
let me say this year I used your money to pay
an Anchorage therapist for a fifty-minute hour.
I'm near through snipping this last frayed thread.

In Knowledge

Mother, you never liked snake,
porcupine, or skunk, strong wind
in your face, the rain, a beach
with no lifeguard, large parties,
intimate friends, chance. Mother,
you never liked grass stains
or sweat, the smell of onion,
redwood, doghouse, sap,
the smell of sex, my father pumping,
grunting, rumbling, coming.

Mother, I never realized how
you made me feel ashamed
to be seen, how I hated
your queer condescending grin,
your arching sneer, your whiny
self-righteous knack, your strange
lack of insight and fight,
your wasted life. Mother,
because I knew nothing of this,
I mirrored you to death.
Now look. I'm cracking glass.

Mother, Mother

My depressed mother never smiled, never
admitted she loved her physical pain,
reckoning symptoms as collectibles, proof
the world noticed. I feel terrible,
yes, she'd mutter. But mother, I'd say.
Really hurts—but I'll drive you, she'd sigh.

My mother, hypochondriac? My mother,
actress? My mother, victim? Yes. Yes.
Regrettably yes—of her own lousy luck.
Terribly insecure, an awkward lonely
youth. Haughty confused adult unsure how
responsibility worked, she chose

martyrdom as another might philately,
opera, architecture. Her talent:
to fill children with guilt, drag them
helplessly down, satisfy her own
emptied swamp. Mother, mother—
really, good-bye. This time for good.

Poem Turning Into a Letter I Will Not Mail

My father would like a relationship.
Seventy years old, he phones sometimes
to talk, though I disappoint him
with my yes's and no's, my reluctance
to be drawn into the intimacy
he seeks. I could tell him, I guess,
to start, that I was in a plane crash
nine months ago, suffered a concussion
from which I haven't yet recovered.
I could mention that I'm $25,000
in Mastercard debt, have little income,
am near the end of my credit line,
am not sure what next (though might
come out well-to-do after a lawsuit),
and live in a small studio apartment
without a kitchen. I could add
that my current home, Juneau, is the capital
of Alaska, and I've found opportunistic
and stubborn men and women
so much like him as I lobby for arts
and education. (And here
I might thank him for teaching me
how best to approach those difficult people.)
I could finish by saying that I've written poems
about him that have been published,
and would hurt him if he was truly mellowed,
and sincerely wanted to know.

On Depression

Bury it, my father said,
the unasked-for advice
his own daily practice,
a quick three-syllable cure.
Bury it. His surface charm
hid headaches, an ulcer,
chronic high blood pressure.

Years ago he quit talking
to his brother, last year
his sister. I'm estranged,
having spent my childhood scared:
who knew when a chance misdeed
struck rot, and out popped
the mean ugly sorehead dad.

Did you hear me son—
I said to bury it.
Turning away, disgusted,
I told him to fuck off.
There. I could handle my funk—
it would pass. His was forever
leaking, boxed deep inside.

Father and Son

To pursue his dream, the father
abandoned a wife, a daughter, and a son
to build a business. Today he lives
in a classy suburb, a fancy house.
Though his second wife dotes, the ex
is shattered, the daughter copes,
and the son, a writer, practices
the craft of killing his old man off
on paper. Dear old Dad.
The father's been choked, hung,
drowned, knifed. He's suffered
sudden heart attacks, drawn-out
cancers, bad luck in cars.
Neglected as a boy, the son
learned to survive
by making the imagined, real.
The father, no better or worse,
never had a chance.

Dear Dad

Forgive my poetry. Though I owe all
to the long ago Philadelphia January
daybreak intimacy that conceived me,
your neglect betrayed: I remain away,
the frostbit son, the one force-fed
through childhood by a frozen mother
who raised me to accept the cold
emptiness of an unlit living room
fireplace, a suburban oblivion.
So long encased in ice, I live alone
in the far north, and write stories
of anger, loss, misery, change.
If only I could be a mature wolf
at play with my pack, or a king salmon
fighting the rough current home.
If only I could release your grip,
your stubborn frowning greed.
If only winter would end.

One or Two Maybes

I can understand how my father—husky,
good-looking, horny—and my mother—
spoiled, brittle, pretty—first
got together: two Jewish singles,
a dark and smoky Catskills dance floor,
a five-piece band playing *Stardust*.
Maybe he offered a cigarette
or a sip of gin. Maybe he touched her,
told her she was beautiful. Maybe
his fingers lingered on her shoulder,
slid down her arm, and she shivered.

I can understand how one or two maybes
turned a frivolous moonlit flirtation
to courtship, and how stupidity
led to a ruinous marriage that lasted
twenty years after the thrown knife,
the sorry apology, the grim and shameful
lovemaking of that Atlantic City honeymoon
all foretold misery. I can understand
placing the blame on the children.
Conscious, maybe, of the way maybes go,
I'm divining the story. Finally.

The Past

He didn't want her
to know he wanted her
for her body.

She didn't want him
to know she wanted him
because he wanted her.

They didn't want each other
to know they needed
each other: to know

they needed.

The Train

1

The pain was bad,
deep like the night
I woke with gas,
crept downstairs
to the encyclopedia,
read the entry, stole
into my mother's bed-
room, and lifted the key.
Holding my belly
so nothing shifted,
I drove through the dark.

They didn't believe me,
but I sat, knowing
the next wave of nausea
would hit like a train.
And it did. Just in time
I wobbled down the hall
to kneel at the toilet
and puke. By 5 A.M.
I was under anesthesia.
When admissions phoned
my mother, I understand
she said: *What on earth?*
My son's right here.

2

Like a second burst appendix.
The pain was *that* bad
in the Salt Lake
train station men's room.
Doubled over, unsure
whether to vomit
or shit, I had to blow
my nose. Thick red

bloody gobs.
A half hour later,
flushing blood, shit,
vomit, I could barely
stand, barely inch out
the tiled bathroom
and across the unswept
lobby, my pack
impossibly heavy,
like I had my mother
and father on my back.
The hard train home.

Which I'd been riding all along.

The Elephant Wars

Finally, it's all the same:
blood and bone, secret
upon secret on top of us
like elephants. One stomp
would do it. Stomp. So
we're stomped on daily.
Listen to the sky creak
from the weight of God,
the big daddy elephant
who runs the scoreboard,
piles corpses at the door.

The Fatality of Light

Dying is the hard part—
the white sky that's too bright
after you climb the high dive
and stand there, ready,
toes on the edge, alive
to death's double somer-
sault: the midair straightening,
the headfirst entry into water.

Being dead is easy—
asleep within the liquid box,
a body peacefully sinks
now knowing its twin,
wings spread like a hawk's
for the dying flight blind-
folded: shiny feathers burning,
the sunlight on fire.

IV

Recipe for Foreboding

Take a cup of chaos, two shakes
of hesitation, sprinkle in discomfort,
disorder, a tiny sound like mice
clatter. Add angst. A distinct
yet not inconsequential piddling
or noodling. A falling. An ending.
A suicide is pending, you hear
a dream voice remark. A pit
in the gut like a broken orchestra
tuning. Or some buried grocery
sinking. Why don't clocks go
tick-tick-tock? Another squeak
passes into another breath,
another bite, another quick taste
of our diminishing. Enough. Enough!

A Miniature Purée

Some nightmare, this urban hocus-
pocus of car horns and jabber,
traffic backed on bridges, traffic
packed with the sober, the waggish,
glam drag queens too, traffic
that flabbergasts, so much rubber
over so much asphalt, the drizzle
of Hiroshima in every commute.
Daily we scrape just to get by.
We sow, we reap, we shove another
disk into the deck, push eject,
take in NPR: socialism, communism,
some new hot spot, the demise
of one more dictator, the rise
of another. This latest jam
is two miles long. Where's the remorse?
Where's the courtesy? We shove
a new CD into the deck, listen
to the novel we have no time
to read, something about a papoose.

Vitamin X

Just *look*. The world's full
of rich, nutritious Vitamin X.
Bite into the moon. Swallow
rivers, oceans, clouds, stars.
Chew through air and earth.
Develop a taste for wind.
Feel better? Keep eating—
most everyone does. Demand
seconds, thirds, fourths.
Minimum daily requirements:
a greedy appetite, a big mouth,
an army of poor slobs to sweep,
mop, haul shit to the dump.

History Class

Ask the wolf on the plate
about famine in Africa.
The answer: Am I
appetizer or dessert?

Ask the salmon in the soup
about poverty in America.
The answer: Am I
a dog to lie?

Ask the tracks by the river
about consensus among men.
The answer: Are we
martyrs or masters?

Ask the hungry moon
about the meaning of time.
The answer: The days
slide onward, tracking us.

Uncle Floyd's Tongue Recipe

If the tongue's fresh,
it'll waddle when you shake it—
or you extracted it
from the head yourself.

Carefully wash the tongue
clean "against the grain"
to eliminate all materials
from grooves and crease.

In a pot large enough
so the tongue can wiggle
as it boils, add celery,
onion, spices. Cook two hours.

Remove tongue from pot
(you can make soup from stock—
though I won't). Believe me,
texture's a bit strange.

Taste will be soft and mild.
Cow tongues tend to be harder
due to use. Personally,
I don't care for tongue.

But you might.

Today's Menu

For breakfast, begin
with disappointments
from the concentrate.
One major loss, a few
new minor ones added.
Next, scrambled symptoms,
sides of confusion, pain,
family lies. Make room
for an accident. Serves
five, all of them you.

For lunch, mutter
and glance at your watch.
Ah, you're not late,
you, the mouth. Funny,
you think, how time
has stopped. You laugh,
and if it wasn't so rude
you'd eat that laugh.
Ask the server to return
in two minutes.

For dinner, the ritual
of sitting at the table
and dipping bread
into soup or sauce,
manipulating forks,
chopsticks, and the rest:
an hour of appetizer,

salad, meat. This is
about grace, not food.
Tomorrow will bring dessert.

Midnight Hungers

Tonight they creep down
stairs that creak comic
as a burp of beer,
a bellyful of beans.
Floorboards that groan
like kids seesawing
between banana splits
and devil's food cakes.
Did I say creep down
stairs? I meant sleep
upon stories. Take
ghosts by the shoulders.
Dream into the light.

Advice for a Single Mom

The next rainy morning pick an orange
marigold from the bed, lick its furls
inside and out, then suck the stem
like a pipe. For one moment forget

the diapers, the crying, the relentless infancy.
Remember the wind. Let it carry you
to the desert and beyond, to the highlands
where clouds and mountains clash. Forget

the father. Forget him. The rain will hold.
Attend the garden. Thin the carrots
and for dinner sauté with ginger
until those orange fingers shine.

By moonlight paint your son's room
blue with yellow halos. Listen for sleep.
Alexander will grow round as a puddle.
Love will deepen, an infinite rippling.

The Waiting Game

Waiter sees waitress
as chef does sauce:
the color, the smell,
the taste, the flame.

Waitress sees waiter
as baker does bread:
the size, the shape,
the dough, the rise.

Waiter and waitress,
professional servers,
mate with patience,
as befits the calling.

Leftovers and Gravy

The end of May, a bright
late afternoon sun slow-bakes
a world hungry to use itself up.

See how we hurry to plant seeds,
build shelters, begin families,
move on. See how we add

an onion, a stairway, a child,
a self. See how we roast
into June, July, August.

See how we taste with gravy.

V

On Being Small

The clouds,
sky, moon,
sun, stars,

remain
that much
further

from finger-
tip reach,
that much

more wondrous.
I remain
intimate

with earth.

A Brief Tour of the Body

Brain

not an egg
not an apple

what the belly
dreams . . .

Bone

Brawny bully.
Exiled baby.
Hungry for
blood. Feeds
on self . . .

Hair

Face it.
We need places
to grow. And
be cut . . .

Smile

Like the moon,
it circles,

circ, ci,
cir, circles . . .

Flesh

Let's make up.
You'll be us.
We'll be you.
Okay? . . .

Groin

struggling
for smarts
a muscle
dancing

atop
apple
seeds . . .

Birthmark

Oh God,
you've made
us mad
and peculiar

as dogs . . .

Haiku Zoo

Ape falling apart.
Now now mad brother monkey—
kiss a little ass.

Bat spreads like the night
through gray February dusk.
Veers sharp left, star-bound.

Coyote laughing
hard in the far hills. Dark moon
eclipses dead sun.

Donkey see, donkey
do, donkey pins its own tail
to meet the shadow.

Elephant used to
feel small. Bathed. Shaved. Found a mate.
Grew big and wrinkly.

Fox heard a voice
within. Ate a frog for lunch.
Now fox croaks ghost tunes.

Giraffe and grizzly
shared a cage. Long spotty husband.
Furry wife. Weird kids.

Hippopotamus
sunning on a blue glacier
gets hypothermic.

Ibex cracks a smile
sliding downhill, exactly
like a horny snake.

Jackrabbit quickly
wiggles, thumps, races, leaps, makes
more busy bunnies.

Kangaroo language:
hip-hop, pop; hip-hop pop; pip-
squeak pop-pops in pouch.

Llama dreams a long
slow pack up Fuji. Ascending
into lavender.

Moose hoof moose hoof moose
hoof clopping across asphalt
moose hoof moose hoof moose

Narwhal and walrus
wrestle underwater, touch
tusks, come up for air.

Owl and ostrich duel.
Winner takes on peacock. Three
feathers out of five.

Porcupine learns words
by removing a large quill,
dipping into ink.

Queen bee buzzed around
for what seemed a century.
Workers come and go.

Rhinoceros out
of its mind. Spends days writing
beastly comedy.

Skunk and shark remake
the old story: Once upon
a smelly fierce time . . .

Turtle finds small stone
on beach. Polishes until
dull mother-of-pearl.

Unicorn points out
that gryphons prefer old gnus
to silly young yaks.

Vulture or vampire?
Inside shallow breath a black-
blooded angel screams.

Wolf in steel trap howls
for help. The pack emerges.
Hundreds of full moons.

—xoxox
ox ox ox ox ox ox ox
(haiku zookeeper)

Yellowsnapper swims
toward surface vision—perhaps
greater yellowlegs.

Zebra paints over
stripes with reds, pinks, violets—
spring's evening twilight.

Gnome

Comic, odd, unlikely, slow—
Nome's practical joker if you will,
A strange little man with mustache
and goatee who each dawn demands
special birthday boy treatment,
pipsqueak orphan of ninety-three.

Today's present, a mirror. Look,
gnome. Your left eye's askew, winking
at the tub where you've soaked
yourself clean—check the dark ring
caked with excuses, rust, ashes, blame.
Look, your right eye's twinkling anew

with the light—some private matter
no doubt, between you, power, wiring,
glass. Past ghost, leprechaun,
elf, watch yourself grow one foot,
two, practically a prince, opening a chest,
pulling out heart, soul, every wish.

Two Scientists Discover Dance

He asks her. Or perhaps she
asks him. Now something sways
as they creep so funny,

a small slow step, another,
a third that's perhaps a skip.
He's the ominous cloud—

she's all sad elegance.
Forward, forward, one
then the other thinks,

the pair almost adept.
A quick imaginary butterfly
or tiny toy bird. Delicate,

delicate now. Surprised
by this music of math,
they waltz quietly out of sight.

For Jan and John

Somewhere between therapy
and upholstery—traditional?
triumphant?—you'll find
a couple—ticklish?
true blue?—who'll confuse you
(and each other). Un-
compromising? Ubiquitous?
Thunderstruck? They'll boggle
you with homespun brilliance,
wit, entwine you in tales
of wilderness trips. A history
of playing music, committed
listening, love. Togetherness?
Yes, togetherness. Hike
any summit, and see.

The Yard

Yesterday's grass,
trampled and mowed,

already returns,
each blade a secret

poem, knowing seed,
root, dirt, luck,

light. The grass
can't help itself.

Nor can the children.
Sunny gnomes awake

to summer's approach,
they peer outside

through bedroom windows,
see a team of angels

tumbling, backflipping,
remounting the yard.

God Logic

They travel every which way—
toward, away from, circling,
zig-zagging, stuck, divided—
a dozen pilgrims en route.

Two work. One threatens.
Two host. One retreats.
Two build. One maintains.
Two keep. One desires.

Breaking out of solid fog
across the bridge, mixing
love with light, a thirteenth
survivor drinks at the well.

Next Journey

Not Guatemala,
El Salvador,
not even Nepal.

Just evening
tapering,
a slow blink

sliding
past midnight,
a blond Jesus

walking toward me,
a skeleton key
his right hand's

middle finger.
I've come
to open Pandora,

I hear,
and wake alert
to the universe.

VI

The Blue Moon Month

Monquapaquoq—a place name
that may or may not mean
Mountain That Shines.
Near the summit, twilight,
a shaman dressed
in fur hat,

parka, gloves, boots,
dances in a ring
of snow, singing
as he juggles three spears,
each point
orange

with flame.
From the spit
hangs a moose carcass,
a bull shot
mid-month, no moon,
an arrow to the heart.

Ascending the mountain,
a woman, pack full
of seeds, beans, clothes,
shepherding a ewe.
She climbs oblivious
to the weight,

the weather.
Her squint
seeks the shaman
near waterfalls and crags,
by creeks and ravines,
in air, wind, rain.

Into the darkness,
juggling fire, it is for her
the shaman sings,

for her the shaman dances.

Machete

I woke today dreaming about a machete—
I don't know if I'll ever learn
to use one. And do I drink enough liquids?
So many people and so much consumption.
But at least I'm learning how to love.
God? I don't know much about god,

but that's okay, because god
can be in poetry. And in a poem, god can handle a machete,
and finds that the god self absolutely loves
the sharpness, the swing, how that god self is learning
to cut with that blade. Maybe that's the consumption
I'm made for: learning through poems. We're air and liquid,

aren't we, though I feel so earthbound, me a liquid
man on a liquid planet. I believe in god
in some poems, not in others. Same with consumption.
In one poem I'll have to take the machete
from my lover, show her how I'm learning
the mystery of bananas and banana trees. How I love

my lover, who can handle both machete and love,
who has made peace with air, earth, ocean. She's liquid
and she's mineral and she's animal and she's learning
how to combine goddess and god
as she takes one more swing with the machete.
She understands consumption

in ways that transcend consumption.
How does she do it? She understands love

in ways that transcend love. She'll take a machete
in a dream, and manage to slice through liquid.
How does she do it? By combining goddess and god
she transcends the past. She's forever learning

what's next. And so I learn
from her because we're lovers, and consumption
is part of what makes us both goddess and god.
We're lovers because of the power of love,
which is sometimes earth, sometimes air, sometimes liquid.
And sometimes it means taking turns with a machete,

and learning how it's a metaphor for love—
so dangerous, and so beautiful in its consumption. Yet it's also liquid—
ask the dream god and goddess as they share the machete.

To My Love

1

Lessons of all kinds
if we're open. This zest
for growth. *Zest*,
tell me what is that
exactly. Every long day

we have this chance
to see how the golden world
operates. There's
more than we know.
Perhaps a glimpse

of some future story
or song. There's always
now, an arriving train.

2

Let me fall into you—
and I'll fall into beauty.
What's this you and I?
A turn to some sacred buzz?
Zippy minutes of sparkly fizz?
I'm learning something, this *I*,
easy music of cello and fiddle.

What do you see? A heart?
Happy fingers and toes?
A wish on a kindly star
that's shooting to mysterious
universes? I'm poor at falling,
so I strive to keep safe.
Then I look again. Your eyes—

oh, that's what I know.
No doubt, I'm falling in.

3

I love her
    mastery of hammer, chisel,
        monkeywrench, screwdriver, axe;
I love her
    embodiment of magic—
        how she can lift her leg into a cloud;
I love
    she's part rattler, part raven,
        part dolphin, part lion, part fox;
I love her
    penchant
        for percussion;
I love
    the grass, the fields, the lakes,
        the sky, the wind are her progeny;
I love
    she's miraculous as fire,
        ritualistic as smoke.

I love
    to say
        I love her.

4

Every day another blessing
lasting until the next. So
it's day after day we sometimes
approach a state so far
beyond grace that we're speechless.

Every day another blessing
that may be big, that may be small,
that we accept, no matter what.

5

Let's imagine
zero—zero
informing everything:

from our origin,
past eternity,
to this,

our infinite,
excellent
roundness.

6

I see you as genius of ritual
who makes every day a ceremony.
Breakfast? Lunch? Dinner? All ceremony.
Sun? Moon? Water? Fire? All consensual
and worthy of song. Always punctual
with spirit. No patience for those phony
men who'll endlessly prattle, their bony
penises guiding them—all so futile.
Oh, my dear, how you make me smile and laugh—
both serious and silly. An artist
and maker. Chatty pal. Best listener.
Sign me up as playmate, lover, the staff
co-producer. Perhaps time for a list
of ingredients. We're the commissioners.

7

Look, listen, smell, taste, touch—then
imagine a sixth sense, some long-desired
space, that improbable special
spot of big cat and placid moose.
Imagine a seventh sense next, dreams
each night tangled in hands and feet,
sometimes an arm or leg draped

between for extra effect.
Imagine an eighth sense next, that endless
river of minutes, hours, months
that can be rapid and crazy, or wide and slow,
happy to be this time of exploration.

Doesn't each day define you?
And doesn't each day define us?
My love, this is a celebration.

8

How we curl
under and over, closer
and closer, relaxed
and tight, bodies
wading step by step
into one another,
no extra spaces,
deepening, deepening,
laughing as we relax
further, snuggle under
and over, letting love
expand so it spills
off our bodies into the air.
Nothing separates us.
Some days are like that.
Some nights are like that.

9

She observes young deer
frolicking with their mothers
in woods or meadows
under summer sky.

Sometimes she finds small rocks
that hold her as she holds them,
so she reaches, examines further,
chooses one or two to bring home.

She is my love on her mission
to observe color, shape, creature,
plant. There she goes: bluebird
taking flight, swollen creek rushing,

fungi poking from leaves.

10

Tell me what it means, everlasting love.
With you, it's a joining every morning
and evening; it's hours of light, or warning;
it's an acceptance of all that's above
and all below; it's the desire to move
as one, sometimes so awkwardly dancing
we laugh and cry; it's a shy romancing
and a long list of groceries to shove
in a pocket; it's you and I, sometimes
becoming so bright, sometimes a deep darkness;
sometimes a trail in woods, the steepest climb
for miles; sometimes alone, a heaviness
that's trying to say one won't live without
the other—profound pain, yes, but not doubt.

On Our Way to Wales

Perfect morning, quintessential England.
Soft sky, shiny sun, two snipes peeping
on the lawn. I'm feeling sharp,
my wife snuggled beside me, her lips
curled her comic way. On her neck
a strawberry where I bit last night—
a fit of sado-masochism in the missionary.

To honeymoon by bicycle on this isle—
warm spring hills, a fair east tail wind,
picnic lunches of mustard and cheese,
endearments in our affected English,
the quaint room here in New Market.
Dearest darling, lovebird sweet, I pray
for nothing save the permanence of our love.

VII

How We Scatter

in memory of Warren Argo

A life may begin in Fresno,
Seattle, maybe Philadelphia,
swing you to Spokane, Juneau,
perhaps Port Townsend. We attend
schools, graduate, take jobs,
quit them, move again. We get
married. Or don't. We have
children. Or not. We make
friends—friends, the existential
as we hug hello, exchange smiles
or tears, waltz ourselves across
continent, feet barely touching floor.

How we scatter as the years
have their way. What's the sound
of an intent engineer steady
on board? A festival of fiddlers
lost in tunes, clawhammer banjos
making clawhammer noise? A proud
dad phoning his girl? What's the sound
of collective joy? How we scatter,
settling from Olympia to Opelousas,
Oakland to Santa Fe to Fairbanks,
finding community ever more fully
in this world. And then the next.

8 or 9 Ways of Hearing Greasy Coat

1

I don't drink
I don't smoke
I don't wear
No greasy coat

Ken Waldman doesn't sing much
but he'll sing this one

2

Sometimes Ken Waldman explains:
a greasy coat is a euphemism
for a condom. He's learned how
to judge audiences. He'll only explain
when he thinks he'll get a laugh.

3

Ken Waldman met a British fiddler,
taught her the tune, sang it,
then defined *greasy coat*. Oh, she said,
I thought it was a raincoat. Yes,
in a way, Ken Waldman answered.

4

It's one of the few times
Ken Waldman plays banjo.
For young children, he calls
the tune Billy Goat, and sings

I don't wink
I don't joke
I don't pet
No billy goat

5

Ken Waldman visited
a university dance class,
played the tune on fiddle,
banjo, then mandolin.
He watched the dancers move
according to the instrument.

6

Go to a computer, type *greasy coat*
in a search engine, add *Augusta*,
find yourself on a happy porch
in Elkins, West Virginia.

7

Wallace Stevens wrote
Thirteen Ways
of Looking at a Blackbird.

Ken Waldman borrowed
the idea to write this.

Or did he steal it?

8

Maybe you've heard this:
Good writers borrow;
great writers steal.

(Ken Waldman doesn't know
how modest to be here.)

9

In Louisiana, a bonus
treat is called *lagniappe*.

This immodest poem always
asks for something more.

Bassoon

for Linda Harwell

Loon music of honks and hooks.
Devil's dearest. Pipe of skunk
     and mushroom, Mozart and moan.
     Skinny silver-and-black balloon.
Blow it up. Classy funk
          goes pop. Tuxedos that chortle
     and cavort. Traditional punk.
     Oxymoronic sport. Who's crying?
Like a doctor cutting open
          a snake. Or an achy swollen
     infected spine. Or a stiff whip.
     Or moon tubing. Or a quick wind
          that croons rueful thirteens.

2020

We're in the year of perfect vision
when you and I fully see
the big decision

about what's next. Our mission
these months: to embrace each week, and be.
We're in the year of perfect vision,

our time to stop feeding the pigeons,
climb with hawks and eagles, soar free.
The big decision—

who was it who said it's all illusion,
the daily clutter that keeps us all so busy?
We're in the year of perfect vision,

each hour an ideal lens for addition,
subtraction, division, whatever feels key
for the big decision

that could propel us to Hawaii, Michigan,
Utah. So perfectly absurd, this surreal surreality
we're in. The year of perfect vision?
2020: the big decision.

In Time of Pandemic

Make plans lightly—
be set to pivot
and slyly

change course. Nightly
re-examine all of it.
Make plans lightly,

mulling alternatives (likely
to sputter or stall). Sit
and slyly

meditate. Ruminate dryly
how we're all in infinite shit.
Make plans lightly,

repeating these are mighty
mystifying times. Savor your wit,
and slyly

(un)mask your own feisty
ways. No coughing. Don't spit.
Make plans lightly,
and slyly.

Angry Man

Impossible to imagine a female,
no matter how angry or desperate,
would have crept across the Radisson lot
at 3 or 4 A.M. with a rock
to smash a passenger side window.
That's man's work, the satisfaction
of a quick shatter of glass,
an otherwise inconspicuous old sedan.
The gamble: inside the small bag
on the front seat, a tablet or camera;
inside the bigger backseat bag,
gadgets and instruments of greater value;
inside the glovebox—a wad of fifties,
or jewelbox of rubies and pearls.
Angry man, you rifled through glovebox
papers: receipts for oil changes,
tire purchases, sundry repairs; you swiped the change
from the beverage holder—dimes, nickels,
pennies totaling less than three bucks; you
tore open the backseat bag to find a mad nest
of bags zippered inside bags; you snatched
that little green satchel on the front seat. Perhaps
you've calculated what you can get
for the twelve paperbacks that were within—
the collected works of Ken Waldman.
Angry man, now you're angrier.

Villanelle for George Floyd

He was a black man—
that matters. The consensus:
a gentle and friendly (if flawed) American,

raised a proud Texan,
murdered in Minneapolis.
He was a black man—

that matters. The same story yet again.
What kind of country is this—
a gentle and friendly (if flawed) American

black man meets his end:
a knee to neck. He wasn't dangerous;
he was a black man—

wrong time, place, color. In
nine minutes, four cops dismissed
a gentle and friendly (if flawed) American

who mattered. *I can't*
breathe, he repeated. What matters is
he was a black man,
a gentle and friendly (if flawed) American.

The Poet Contemplates Datacide

This might be what happens when you die,
a shock so sickening and sad. The whole
world now emptied of those you know. It's all
gone, all of it, plain done, good-bye good-bye
to in-box, sent mail, drafts. You can ask why,
but what's the satisfaction of "firewalls
breached," "fried servers," "freak bugs." No peace at all—
your back-up, too, vanished in some cloud. Why?
Why? Twelve years of work. Twenty thousand names.
The record of your days on computer—
the proposals, the stories, the numbers—
all threads now passed to memory, a lame
airy vault. You recall a deceased friend's
last email, her brave struggle to the end,
the specifics now yours to reinvent.
Some day, true, you'll be going where she went.
For now the long task of making amends:
type an address, craft a note, add poem, press *Send.*

Halloween, 2020

This dark year—
long lonesome days
of virus and fear:

masks began to appear
most everywhere by May.
This dark year

has been part bear,
skunk, dragon, always
the virus and fear.

Trick or Treat! Another gear
has slipped, COVID to stay
this whole dark year

and next. It's clear,
the ghouls behind tonight's play
of virus and fear.

The doorbell rings. It's here—
it's not going away,
this dark year
of virus and fear.

November 1, 2020, Floyd, Virginia

So much has changed. The very strangest time,
these months, as we've altered our basic ways.
Seven days are still a week, but now a maze
of odd activities, temporary rhyme,
unexpected reason. Though fifteen dimes
still make a buck fifty, and thirty days,
November, Thanksgiving will be sideways—
Christmas plain crazy. We want a straight line
where there is none. This shrewd killer virus
fills the news, pays no mind to national
politics. It doesn't care about us
in the least. It feels so irrational,
stealth messenger of sickness and death.
Our autumn to be still, ruminate, breathe.

2021

We're thankful
the past year is done.
It was near impossible,

wasn't it, improbable
virus amid remarkable corruption.
We're thankful

2020 is kaput. Such trouble,
wasn't it, twelve-month junction
that was near impossible

to navigate, a climate we're not yet capable
to fully re-imagine.
We're thankful

that with so much abnormal,
we're still here, you and I (even
in what may be near impossible

circumstances), we resourceful,
phenomenal, irrepressible humans.
We're thankful.
2020 was near impossible.

Detroit Sestina with Coda

Somewhere in Detroit
a woman is going into labor.
She may be rich.
She may be poor.
She may be in a car
(after all, this is Detroit—

and we all know Detroit,
don't we?). Ah, Detroit.
Blight. Poverty. Motown. Cars.
Walter Reuther. Labor.
Pistons. Lions. Tigers. Rich
lakefront communities. Poor

people in drafty homes poring
over coupons to buy food. Detroit
has Whole Foods. The rich
buy organic grapefruit. Detroit
has history. Middle-class labor
built an America of cars,

turnpikes, bridges, tunnels. The car
is king. Even the poor
have cars. All of us labor
to make a paycheck last. Detroit
has labored to make its payroll. Detroit,
where bankruptcy lawyers get rich.

Lansing politicians also get rich.
And D.C. lobbyists in chauffeured cars.
They all take from Detroit.
What do they offer in return? Poor
Detroit. Humble, beautiful Detroit.
Hard-working motor city laboring

to make ends meet. Labor
made Detroit prosper. Rich
and innocent middle-class Detroit
might have been Manhattan. Cars
and taxis. Even the poor
felt rich in that Detroit.

What happened? The labor of making cars
gave birth to the poor entitled rich
that bled Detroit—the old Detroit.

(Somewhere in Detroit
a woman is going into labor.
She may be rich.
She may be poor.
She may be in a car.
That child will unite Detroit.)